943

Gift

University of St. Francis
GEN   811.5 F295b
Feeney
Boundaries

3 0301 00027320 7

D1280326

BOUNDARIES

THE MACMILLAN COMPANY
NEW YORK · BOSTON · CHICAGO · DALLAS
ATLANTA · SAN FRANCISCO

MACMILLAN & CO., LIMITED
LONDON · BOMBAY · CALCUTTA
MELBOURNE

THE MACMILLAN COMPANY
OF CANADA, LIMITED
TORONTO

BOUNDARIES

BY

LEONARD FEENEY, S.J.

NEW YORK

THE MACMILLAN COMPANY

1936

LIBRARY
College of St. Francis
JOLIET, ILL.

Copyright, 1935, by

THE MACMILLAN COMPANY.

All rights reserved—no part of this book
may be reproduced in any form without
permission in writing from the publisher,
except by a reviewer who wishes to quote brief
passages in connection with a review written
for inclusion in magazine or newspaper.

Set up and printed.

Published September, 1935.

Reprinted October, 1935; April, 1936.

PRINTED IN THE UNITED STATES OF AMERICA
BY THE STRATFORD PRESS, INC., NEW YORK

811.5
F295b

Causa nostrae laetitiae,
ora pro nobis.

February 12, 1943 – Newman (Bookshop) Berkeley – 1.25

17144

CONTENTS

BOUNDARIES

BOUNDARIES

Over us and under
Is a world of wonder:
In between we blunder,
Blunder in between
The unseen and unseen,
And on someone's word
Hear of the unheard.
From our faiths and hopes
In prophets and in popes,
And in microscopes,
Mites and sprites we know
Are above, below,
And vice versa so.

Amœbas and archangels
Send us their evangels:
In between the ropes
Where we stand and stare
At the empty air;
Seeing only sights
That are lit by lights,
Hearing only sounds
That are kept in bounds
By celestial sheriffs
On their ghostly rounds
In between the seraphs
And the fleas on hounds.

[1]

ADVICE TO VERSE-MAKERS

It is not information
That causes inspiration.

There are no lambs and Marys
In any dictionaries;

And no beanstalks and Jacks
In any almanacs.

Beauty's a thing to earn
More than a thing to learn.

It comes from simply seeing
The sharp bright point of being,

Whose vein of gold is struck
By labor linked with luck.

And when a rapture fills
The auricles and ventricles

And gives the mouth through art
Connection with the heart,

One can assign the season,
But never knows the reason.

DIAGRAM

Elbows and knees are mysteries
   Of which I become aware,
Dwindled at night to half my height
   And folded up in prayer.

Where do they go? I do not know,
   When on my bed I've laid me;
Crooked or straight may I give great
   Glory to God Who made me.

Let not my little Muse
Deceive you or confuse.
Not in the pose of art
Do I disclose my heart;
Nor do I use to pray with
The poems that I play with.
Rhyme is my little toy
To make-believe with and enjoy.

Not listening in shells
For the booming of beaches
No tide ever swells,
No ship ever reaches,
Do I pretend to find
Foundation for my mind.

I loathe the aesthetic attitude,
The literary languish,
The anguish after anguish,
The hunger for hunger, not for food,—
The joy that is not jolly,
The making tears a trade,
The professional melancholy,
The fear of being afraid.
I hide my whole head under
The sheets when I hear thunder.

Things and not theories
Frighten and make me freeze.

[4]

And, by the way,
Speaking of how to pray,
Dogmas come first, not liturgies.

The dilettante hand
That took art seriously,
That outlawed fairyland
And stripped the Christmas tree,
Now tries another trick
And has revived Our Lord
To go with the candle-stick
It has so long adored.
Of Faith it finds a clue
In hyphenated points of view,
Whose novelty is never new,
And whose waste-land has got
A penny watering-pot
Filled up with drops of dew.

A doubt is still a doubt,
Even turned inside out.

Truer tonight to me
Is one small factual flea,
Whose stinging certainty
Impressed upon my nose
Is not a poem, or a pose.

Their noses are assailed with smells,
Their ears are beat upon by bells,
They see the outward coverings
And watch the surfaces of things,
And relish to a slight degree
The savory and unsavory,
And knock their knuckles lightly on
A door or two, and then are gone.

Explore a clue or think it through—
They find it too fatiguing to.
Their yearnings all in yawnings end
Who never to one fact extend
The simple courtesy of wonder,
That rends more reverently asunder
The lips, and makes the mouth let go
A less unpleasant "Ah!" and "Oh!"

If Beauty be but bubble-fair,
A breath of soap-surrounded air
That bounces briefly like a ball
And makes a moisture on a wall,
Then must we leave them to their senses
And save our own intelligences.
Though Christ Himself be whelmed in wheat,
They could not taste, so would not eat.

REGINA COELI

Our single entrant in the race
Of getting hailed as full of grace
Outscored the angels, took the prize,
And won all honors in the skies.

From Revelation one infers
She had no close competitors:—
So Gabriel declared when he
Announced the news upon his knee.

No grudged encomium did he give,
And spared no wild superlative
Acclaiming her whose blood and breath
Was native to our Nazareth.

Beyond the level and the line
Where stars explode and suns decline,
Where moons and meteors cease to whirl,
Our little globe enthroned a girl.

Were there no Mary, this would be
A jungle poem probably,
Writ by a Zulu babbling rhymes
To snakes in sultry summertimes.

THE WHISTLER

Seldom the soaring rocket-light will rise
Up from the flaming heart and reach the eyes.
Often the song of ecstasy, half-sung,
Will find no footing and fall back in the lung.
But one sweet bird up-warbling from the south
Will never miss the mouth.
The whistler's way is best, the school-boy's scheme:
The simple O that pipes away the steam
Lightly escaping from a lonely dream.

THE MOTH

The little muslin moth,
Whose food is flame and cloth,
Flitting in rapid flight
From clothes-closet to light,
In its intense desire
To be dissolved in fire,
Many manœuvres made
Around my red lamp-shade,
That so enchanted me—
To it I faithfully
Promise appropriate praise
In my verse, one of these days,
As soon as I can get,
And put on paper down,
Some nimble epithet
And little noiseless noun.

THE DONKEY

I saw a donkey at a fair
When sounds and songs were in the air;
But he no note interpreted
Of what the people sang or said.

Hitched by a halter to a rail
He twitched his ears and twirled his tail;
In every lineament and line
He was completely asinine.

Though I had heard in local halls
Some eulogies on animals,
I thought it would be utter blindness
To show him any sort of kindness.

It seemed to me that God had meant
To make him unintelligent,
And wanted us to keep our places,
I in my clothes, he in his traces.

And so I turned my mind to things
Like banners, balls, balloons and rings,
For which I had to pay my share
And went on purpose to a fair.

But down the mid-ways while I went
On all the pageantry intent,
I stopped, and started to remember
A little stable in December,

Battered by wind and swathed in snow,
Nearly two thousand years ago,
When one poor creature like to this
Saw Mary give her Child a kiss.

So back I sauntered to the rail,
And stared at him from head to tail,
And gave his cheek a little pat,
And merely let it go at that.

THE ROSE

Perfume and petal
  Are qualities
That test love's mettle
  With too much ease.

Bramble and briar
  Will soon discover
Who is the liar
  And who the lover.

THE WHALE

Out in the bay arose a whale;
And in a flash from surf to sight,
From far-off wave to steamer-rail,
A whale a millionth of its size
Was matrixed in a beam of light,
And wriggled nimbly through my eyes—
Then plunging wildly in my brain
Became enormous once again.

Somewhere a whale is still in motion,
Lashing an ocean in a notion;
He dives through breaker, brine and billow,
Locked in a skull upon my pillow.
How such a wondrous whale can be
Remains a mammoth mystery;
But I must let him splash and spout
Till deep sleep dries his image out.

THE BEE

God to some
Sticky stuff
Not yet alive
In a hive,
Said, "Come! Hum!
Glorify Me!
Be My bee
And buzz
As I bid!"
And sure enough,
It was!
And it did!

RABBIT

Rabbit's eyes are pink,
And they are, I think,
Less to watch with than to wink
With: they are ornamental:
Sight in them is incidental.
All sensation goes
In through rabbit's ears and nose.
Rabbit runs around
With jump and rebound,
Sniffing every sound,
Listening to the light
Falling on the clover.
Rabbit wants to be afraid:
He delights in fright,
And is soft all over.
He is lovable and white,
And by God was made,
So it seems to me,
More for virtue than utility,—
Out of man some tenderness to take:
Just for pity's sake.

On my way to the coops,
  On my way from the pens,
As I was going over
  From the pigs to the hens,

I met a small object
  Of not any use:
A poor, little, pin-feathered,
  Baby-girl goose,

Who was on her way back
  From the hens to the pigs,
And was paddling in puddles
  And treading on twigs,

And who left me enchanted
  From then till I die
With the pretty gold picture
  She put in my eye.

SNAILS

Snails obey the Holy
Will of God slowly.

A RIDDLE

A shower of silver,
   A shower of gold:
But you cannot guess why
   Till the riddle is told.

In a yard in New Hampshire
   In a shower of rain,
I chucked at some chickens
   A shower of grain.

ORTHOGRAPH

In my figurative furbelow, figurative frill,
I was sitting one evening, as old poets will,
And unrolling a parchment and inking a quill,
When a lightning-bug dropped on my window-sill.

And this cheap little modern-American blighter
Kept flicking the flint in his cigarette-lighter;
But because by a trifle my room became brighter,
I tapped him this tune on my tin typewriter.

THE FEATURE FEATURE

The owl is meant to emphasize
Especially the art of eyes.

The elephant's long rubber hose
Insists upon the art of nose.

The ostrich runs around and begs
Attention for the art of legs.

The art of neck belongs to the
Giraffe quite unmistakably.

The pretty peacock will prevail
In making known the art of tail.

The elk extends its chandeliers
To crown the lovely art of ears.

The art of mouth is obvious,
Due to the hippopotamus.

The art of chin is left to man,
Assisted by the pelican.

ADMIRING MAURA

The metaphysics of a dimple
Is rather more involved than simple.

But when she smiles, at seven weeks,
Two pretty nothings in her cheeks

Make Maura most admired where she
Is Maura most reluctantly.

For nature capers most with grace
Through unfulfillments in her face;

And one sees most to rave about
By looking at what God left out.

Two feet long and one foot wide:
But no more Maura on either side!
No more Maura above, below—
Maura begins at that downy hair,
Maura extends to that tiny toe!
No more Maura wherever you go:
Round and round in the fathomy air,
England or China or anywhere;
No more Maura in any place
Save in this limited little space!
But oh, what infinite condescensions
Heaven has made to this crib's dimensions!
Satan has measured a hole in Hell;
But Mother Mary is watching well,
Jesus remembered the day He died,
The Holy Spirit has sanctified:
Two feet long and one foot wide.

SONG OF INDIA

Maura has come to the rubber age:
Turned, so to put it, a rubber page;
Wants to be rolling a rubber ball,
Wants to be squeezing a rubber doll;
Floats in her bath-tub a rubber fish:
All of her playthings are rubberish;
Chews on a red rubber teething-ring;
And when she goes out for a ride in spring,
A noiseless nurse-maid on rubber heels
Perambulates her on rubber wheels.
And lately a cute rubber cold she took,
And sneezed—God bless us!—like this: "Caoutchouc!"

EXPERIMENT

All one needs to say
Is, "Where's the little kitty? . . .
The one you loved so well,
That wore a silver bell? . . .
And did it run away? . . .
Well isn't that a pity!"

And shut will go the eyes
Till memory supplies
The pleasure of the purr,
The rhythm of the fur,
The tinkle in the ears,—
The trickle of the tears.

COMPUTATION

Betty tried hard to do
All that God asked her to,
Which, being such and such,
Was not so very much,
Nor would be much again,
Seeing she died at ten.

And of that half a score,
Three years or little more
Were all she really spent
Being intelligent—
By which I mean to say,
In an authentic way.

From that three take a third
For sleep: upon my word,
This leaves but two years out
Of ten to talk about!

Divide that two in half
To let her play and laugh,
Run errands for her mother,
And mind her little brother:
Then cut from that schedule
Almost a year for school,—
How long a period
Have we got left for God?

17144

LIBRARY
College of St. Francis
JOLIET, ILL.

Allow this little maid,
When she knelt down and prayed,
Some suitable subtractions
For her small mind's distractions:—
Maybe *one day* is all
One could compose and call
Strictly devotional.

Peace, darling!, do not frown
Looking from Heaven down
At my crude computation
Of your sweet soul's salvation!

One day was quite enough;
Blow out your candle—puff!—
That burnt so pure and bright
One morning, noon and night,
And gave for God's delight
Twenty-four hours' worth
Of perfect praise on earth!

HILARION

Bath-robed, slippered, collar-less,
Face unshaven, feet on fender,
Groggy now for good I guess,
Bent in body, spent in splendor:
O my poor Hilarion,
Where has all your glory gone?
Prim and proper in your prime,
Handsome once upon a time,
Rollicking, but never rude,
Proud, but not a prig or prude,
Somewhat in your day a dude,—
Now you sit in solitude,
Curled up by the kitchen fire,
Dressed in dowdiest attire,
Dead in dreams and in desire.

Come, my gay Hilarion,
Put your silken top-hat on!
Do not let untidiness
Desecrate your last distress.
Pin another sweet-to-smell
Rosebud on your coat lapel!
Polish up those Sunday-best
Silver buttons on your vest!
Go and get your cuffs and cane;
Wear your goat-skin gloves again;
Make a flourish till you die
With your spats and spotted tie!

Stand up and unfurl your banners!
Meet death with your nicest manners!
Be a dandy, live or dead;
Send your calling card ahead:
Let the anxious angels know
They will soon behold a beau,
Slick and sleek at sixty-seven,
Strutting down the streets of Heaven!

AFTER THE SHOWER

After the shower I went abroad:
All the wells in the world were full;
Lightning elapsed in the goldenrod,
Thunder subsided inside the bull.
Worms were soaking above the sod;
Lambs regamboled and birds resang.
God flung a violet boomerang,
Arched the ocean from coast to cape,
And, oh, it was gorgeous again to gape
At Hope set up in a horse-shoe shape!

PROMENADE

It is not wise to dally with despair.
It should be promptly taken out to air—
Follow the route from here to Railroad Square.
A corner constable is there to view
Gesticulating gorgeously in blue.
A muscular mechanic may be seen
Inflating tires or pumping gasoline.
A pencil-seller will intrigue the mind
To guess if he be bogus or be blind.
A splendid shiner of unpolished shoes
Will block your hat and fill your head with news.
And when you pass her papa's peanut-stand
Where small Maria, lollipop in hand,
Sticks out her sticky tongue at peevish faces,
Your grudges, grumpinesses, griefs, grimaces,
Will melt like butterscotch, and be beguiled
By the sure, sharp, sweet satire of a child.

MELODY IN A MEAT MARKET

When Billy, the butcher-boy,'s meat-chopping instrument
  Chipped off the tip of his thumb,
At that very moment did Lily, the pantry-maid,
  In for a cutlet come;

And stanching the wound with her clean linen hand-
     kerchief,
  Skilfully bandaged and bound it,
And tearing a strip from her pretty white pinafore
  Wrapped it around and around it;

And stoutly refusing to cheapen her charity,
  Paid for the chop she was buying.
And if this little incident isn't poetical,
  Maybe I ought to stop trying.

IN THE ANTIQUE SHOP

There was a lady made of gold,
And at an auction she was sold.

She was a little lady wrought
In metal moulded by a thought,

And had a faultless face, a form,
A gesture, an extended arm,

And in a mirror on a shelf
She pointed proudly at herself

As if to say to someone: "See,
What a man's mind has made of me!"

"Take her away!", the auctioneer
Bawled to a bidder in the rear,

A grand dame in a gaudy gown
Who paid a hundred dollars down,

And called her limousine and rolled
Off with the lady made of gold.

And oh, I wonder after that
What in the world she pointed at!

THE LILY

While candles on the altar-shelf
   Between the ferns and flowers
Were burning, and the Carmelites
   Chanted the Little Hours:—

Putting her holy woolens on,
   Her sandals and her veil,
Young Sister Mary of the Snows
   Knelt at the altar-rail,

And ceased forevermore to be
   The harbor-dredger's daughter—
The man who digs the murky mud
   From underneath the water.

I cannot go it—go it you who can:
The celluloid survival of a man;
The play that is acted
With the actor extracted;
The counterfeited rapture rolling on;
The surface saved and all the substance gone;
The passion still preserved that no one feels;
The fruit in lemon skins and orange peels.

NOEL

(a Christmas carol by a British playwright)

A stupid horse and cow, they say,
    Called for convenience, ox and ass,
Stood in a stable munching hay:
    A rather stupid sort of grass.

It seems a village girl was there:
    A rather stupid sort of maid,
Whose husband was a carpenter:
    A rather stupid sort of trade.

Her child was lying in a stall:
    A rather stupid place to sleep;
And stupid shepherds came to call
    With stupid lambs and stupid sheep.

The angels sang, *et cetera,*
    Some songs of this world and the next,
And so fulfilled from Isaiah
    A rather stupid sort of text.

HAIR RIBBONS

When we were young, we looked on them as creatures
Inalterable in nature, as in form and features;
Diffidently to be approached, and shyly to be attended,
Extravagantly to be admired, and valiantly to be defended.

We needed no vile diagrams, being not such fools;
Innocence was not yet outlawed in primary schools.
With swift clean flashes of thought we were able to sense
What was their similarity, and what their difference.

And in order to make this clear distinction clearer,
And preserve those distances that keep the genders
dearer,
They wore bright symbols of their strict inalterability:
Hair ribbons they wore, who were, yet who were not as
we.

Manners have gone to the dogs since the hair ribbons departed;
Song is not sweet, nor verse versatile, nor folks openhearted.
There is a blur in the eye, and the mind is annoyed
By a mania, and the ear by a monosyllable inaccurately
employed.

Now what's the good looking like good-looking lasses
Who are just as good-looking in looking-glasses,
Or caring for curls that can be cultivated
Electrically, or voices that can be duplicated
On discs? . . .

LIKE AND LOVE

I know that God is infinite,
But like Him not that way a bit;
I love Him, yes, but like Him less;
God is too big for me, I guess.

But not too little, no siree!,
In Mary's arms, on Mary's knee;
For then I like Him even more
Than I had loved Him heretofore.

INDIGNATION

The inn that would not bed and board
The Blessed Mother of Our Lord,
That night when it had ought, when she
Was most in need of hostelry—
I think I would not pay a pin
To stop at such a stupid inn.
I think it was a dive, a den;
I hereby scourge it with my pen.

EPIPHANY

Now the King-less Jews, I guess,
  Are check-mated,
And their little game of chess
  Terminated.
Two white kings and one black
The Gentiles used in their attack.

APOLOGY

God give me strength
  In making a rhyme
To limit the length,
  To stop it in time.

I could not absorb it,
  Suppose it a star,
If out of its orbit
  It wandered too far.

I could not console it,
  Suppose it a grief,
I could not control it
  Unless it be brief.

COWARDINATION

In little tasks of daily life
   Which every man must do,
Like climbing up and down a hill,
   Or counting two and two,

There are so many ins and outs
   In one's anatomy,
So many wires to be pulled
   And levers to set free,

If I did not have faith in God
   To regulate me right,
I think I'd jump from Brooklyn Bridge
   And finish me in fright.

RETORT TO A PHILOSOPHER

If in future I my lyre
  Ever from its rack remove,
And go plucking with my plectrum
  Anything I cannot prove,

May God lodge me with logicians
  Ranting rhymes and writing reams
Of sweet ratiocinations
  In romantic enthymemes.

DILEMMA

My prayers for you, alas, are all
Somewhat anthropological.
I cannot separate a whole,
Dissect a substance and see a soul;
For when I try, to my dismay
Your anxious eyes get in the way.
I pray you, pray for me when I pray—

Lest I, endeavoring to exclude
Distractions from my solitude,
Disintegrate you far too well,
Halve you and leave you half in Hell.
Before you vanish into air,
May memory salvage one bright hair
Entangled always in my prayer.

THE FAIRYLAND

All that enters through my eye
My intellect must simplify;

For nothing in my mind can be a
Guest unless it's an idea:

A spiritual accident
That has no weight and no extent.

For I am half an angel and
Must alter what I understand,

And rid it of the stubborn stuff
That makes it hard or makes it tough,

And turn its essence into air,
And hoard it underneath my hair.

But if some night my intellect
Should fail its function and neglect

To give some object, as it ought,
The proper lightness of a thought,—

Oh, how I'd toss around in bed
With moons and mountains in my head!

Oh, how I'd yell aloud in pain
With bulls and boulders in my brain!

REFUSAL TO CAST THE FIRST STONE

If in the sin you now confess
There was one tithe of tenderness;

If some sweet charity lay hid
Between your purpose and what you did;

If in this sad iniquity
Childlike you were, or sisterly,

Caught by some subtlety of chance,
Victim of merciless circumstance;

If Jesus may plead at the Judgment Seat:
You were less wicked than indiscreet,

Compassing more than your heart intended;
If you were lonely or undefended;

If one small rampart of your will
Fought against Hell and resisted still,

And one white atom of your soul
Was left unsullied and clean and whole:—

Over that atom, you understand,
I lift up no absolving hand.

Lest I should ever be mistaken for a mad Manichaean,
  Who am enamored of realities maybe not three-dimen-
      sioned enough,
I hereby praise God loudly for all measurements and ma-
    terials,
  Foliage, flesh, fabric and fibre, substance and stuff.

I praise Him for the volatile violets in little convent con-
      servatories,
  For the innocent odors of lilies and the pure aromas of
      roses,
Which even the most ethereal Port Royalists may inhale
      without scruples,
  May sniff with their delicate nostrils and enjoy with
      their noses,

And then go back to the moulding and minding of their
      nuns and their novices,
  Undaunted, unsullied, unruffled, unshriven, unabashed
      and unblamed,
Knowing they have done nothing to violate any one of
      the Commandments,
  Knowing they have done absolutely nothing of which
      to be ashamed.

PIANISSIMO

My meagre brightness must I dim:
  Curtail my scanty skill;
My little well, below the brim,
  In mercy must I fill;

Lest in their folly my sweet friends
  Should think it might be so,
That anything I say portends
  Which way the wind will blow.

The night before Our Lord was born
Saint Joseph went about forlorn,
Knocking at doors from left to right,
Knocking at every door in sight,
Asking if anybody would,
Oh please, would anyone be so good
As to invite the Virgin Mary
In somebody's house that night to tarry—
And had they a room to spare where she
Could wait for Our Lord's Nativity?
But poor Saint Joseph was quite unable
To find a lodging, except a stable;
And it was stuffy and cold and damp,
It had no window, it had no lamp,
It had no table, no bed, no chairs,
It had no up-stairs and no down-stairs;
A very unsuitable place it was,
Inhabited by an ox and an ass;
But they were polite to Our Blessed Mother,
They stood beside her and made no bother,
And did not utter a bray or a moo
Until the time it was proper to,
When the moon went down at the break of morn,
And Christmas began, and Our Lord was born.
And Our Lord was beautiful to behold
The minute He was one minute old.
And He smiled, but of course He did not speak,
He was too little, He was too weak;

But He did do all that He was required:
He lay in the manger and was admired,
And was most worthy to be adored,
For really and truly He was Our Lord!

A PRAYER FOR PROTESTANTS

May God be kind to captive fish
Who dwell in little bowls and wish
To swim, and can't, and have no notion
Of what has happened to the ocean.

And may He bless in aviaries
Continually caged canaries,
Who wonder, when they try to fly,
What can have happened to the sky.

TO ONE CREATED

There are three persons I admire tremendously and love
    the most,
And these are God, The Father, The Son and The Holy
    Ghost.

I admire them the most because beyond all others they
    are
Most personable and permanent and admirable,—much
    more admirable by far

Than you, or than me, or than what-you-may-call-him,
    or so-and-so.
We all are technically persons, we are persons of sorts, I
    know:

But we have no names, save arbitrary tags; and so little
    are we needed
That our loss to existence, if we were to vanish, would
    hardly be heeded.

I agree, to be sure, we are not to blame for it: I grant
    you that,—
Any more than the earth can be blamed for being round
    instead of being flat.

But, not to deserve to be blamed for not having a thing,
    is not
A very good measure of what we are lacking and what
    we have got.

I admit, furthermore, there is indubitably something to
    revere
In many of your attractive and temporal qualities, my
    contingent dear.

But if you and your glories are mutable and mortal, then
    it cannot be odd
That I do not allow you to shine in my eyes like the
    glory of God:

Whose triune, personal splendor my mind by the favor
    of Faith has conceived;
And Who lived and was lovable before any of us loved
    Him, or before He ever needed to be believed.

MEMENTO FOR MY MOURNER

Think you, if this were I,
You would be let to cry?

Were it I, for your sake,
Think you I would not wake?

Ever did you appear
And I not know you near?

When have you found me such,
Cold as a stone to touch?

Seemed I in any mood
Blank as a block of wood?

Gave you I no more heed,
When, than a withered weed? . . .

When, than a lock of hair
Under a barber's chair?

THE DUEL

One of us must surrender
   Ere this affair is done.
I beg You—for it could not be—
   That You be not the one.

Deliriums are delightful
   To soothe a strange disease.
My substance soon will recognize
   Its bare necessities.

Hump me like a hunchback,
   Or trip me on the stairs,
A darling ghost I used to know
   Will prop me with her prayers.

Twist me on Your anvil
   To any shape you know,
For Your instruction I'll protest
   And groan at every blow.

To let You know what costs me,
   What is and is not pain,
From now until the duel ends
   I promise to complain.

Pray for the fragile daughter
  And the frail infant son,
Whom, at the font, the Baptismal water
  I pour upon.

The cycle has swung to sorrow,
  Our ranks have begun to fail;
We know not what gate of Hell tomorrow
  Will not prevail.

The foam-at-the-mouth is frothing
  In the Beast with the flashing tooth;
The Hound that was sent on the scent of Nothing,
  Has found the Truth.

The guns will be hard to handle
  In the forts we will soon forsake.
Pray for the light of the single candle
  On the birthday cake.

MISERERE

One's faith has little nightmares
 It easily survives:—
Divorcing lust and Luther,
 Henry and lots of wives.

But these are sham encounters
 Quickly dissolved in air;
The soul beset no more than this
 Will never know despair.

But oh, to go by moonlight
 And wrestle all alone,
And fight against no heresy
 Except against one's own;

And be entrapped forever
 By what one knows is true,
And dared to do the only thing
 That one desires to do!

This is what makes one falter
 And waver like a wraith;
This is the Christian's agony,
 And this the Faith.

To face those stark alternatives:
 A Nothing and an All;
To choose a Vision or a Void,
 A Silence or a Call;—

This is what sets one groaning
Under the olive trees,
Bathed by the blood of Jesus
In wild Gethsemanes.

THREE SOLDIERS

Three soldiers rose up from their tents
And went to join their regiments.

And one said: "Captain, I report
Because I think that war is sport!"

And one said: "Captain, I am here
Because my duty makes it clear."

And one said: "Captain, I'm afraid
I was not for a soldier made."

So one in fervor, one in fun,
And one in fright took up a gun.

Three soldiers step for step went forth
And wheeled from south to west to north,

And while they marched with drums and tunes
Respectively in their platoons,

Beneath three helmets one could trace
A grinning, grave, and groaning face.

Three soldiers lay upon their backs
When bombs came down on bivouacs

And wildly bursting in the air
Destroyed all soldiers everywhere.

So one for pleasure, one for pride,
And one for love a soldier died.

FINALE

When the Angel has blown on his trumpet a rat-a-tat-
    tat,
And the final encounter of armies is finished and fought;
When the ultimate wire has been snapped on the ulti-
    mate rat,
And the ultimate saucer been licked by the ultimate cat;
When the last little flower has pined in the last little pot,
And the last little ditty has come to the last little dot,—
I will surely be happy—who wouldn't?—at that being
    that;
Though I wonder if really I will be as much as I ought.

THE PYGMIES

I count my pygmies, one by one,
The nearly finished, half-begun,
Bedraggled poems I have written,
Companioned by a clock and kitten,
On littered desk, by candle-light,
Locked in my chamber late at night,
When folks in bed were long tucked in,
And maybe I had better been.